THE GREAT WALL OF CHINA

THE HOOVER DAM

MESA VERDE

THE CH'IN TOMB

MACHU PICCHU

THE WORLD OF
ARCHITECTURAL
WONDERS

Mike Corbishley

PETER BEDRICK BOOKS

Published by
PETER BEDRICK BOOKS
A division of NTC/Contemporary Publishing Group, Inc.
4255 West Touhy Avenue, Lincolnwood (Chicago), Illinois, 60712-1975 USA

Published by agreement with Macdonald Young Books Ltd, England

Designer: Robert Wheeler
Illustrator: Mike Foster and Carl Venton, Maltings Partnership
Commissioning editors: Tom Keegan/Fiona Courtenay-Thompson
Editor: Claire Llewellyn
Picture research: Sandie Huskinson-Rolfe (Photoseekers)

Picture acknowledgements:
The publisher would like to thank the following for allowing their
pictures to be reproduced in this book:

Ace Photo Agency 23 (Peter Noble); Ancient Art and Architecture Collection 19, 28; Aspect Picture Library 37
(top, Tom Nebbia), 40 (Larry Burrows); The Bridgeman Art Library 14 (The British Museum), 32
(The National Gallery); British Museum 32 (right), 33 (bottom); Britstock – IFA Ltd 18 (Bernard Ducke);
Peter A Clayton 20 (P. Clayton); Mike Corbishley 36 (M. Corbishley), 37 (bottom, M. Corbishley); Editions
Valoire – Blois 29; English Heritage Photographic Library 9 (top); J Allan Cash Photo Library 39 (top), 39
(bottom); James Davis Travel Photography 41; Pictor International 9 (bottom), 15, 26; Popperfoto 43 (bottom);
Robert Harding Library 11 (bottom, John Ross), 27 (Gavin Hellier); The Telegraph Colour Library 33 (top);
Tony Stone Images 22; Viewfinder Colour Photo Library 21; Zefa Pictures 11 (top), 17 (Scholz), 43 (top).

Library of Congress Cataloging-in-Publication Data

Corbishley, Mike
    The world of architectural wonders/Mike Corbishley.
        p.   cm.
    Simultaneous published in England as: Superstructures, building
the world's great monuments.
    Includes index.
    Summary: Examines the stories behind such wonders of the world's
architecture as the pyramids of Giza, the Great Wall of China,
Chartes Cathedral, the city of Venice, and Hoover Dam.
    ISBN 0-87226-279-0
    1. Structural engineering—Juvenile literature.   2. Building.
Stone—Juvenile literature.   [1. Structural engineering.
2. Architecture.]   I. Title
TA634.C67   1996
720–dc21   96–47596
                                                      CIP
                                                      AC

Printed and bound by: Ediçoes ASA in Portugal
Endpapers: Map by Peter Bull
Small Artworks by Mike Foster and Carl Venton, Maltings Partnership

Second printing, 1998

Contents

Stonehenge

SALISBURY PLAIN

Stonehenge

Salisbury

Southampton

River Avon

Stonehenge is the most famous stone circle in the world. It was built about 5,000 years ago by a community of farming people who must have been very well organized to construct something so amazing. But what was it for? We think that it may have been used as a temple for ceremonies and religious rituals. The great circular bank around the outside, and the stones themselves, were positioned carefully to exact measurements. They may have been used as a gigantic calendar to record and predict the Sun's path and the changing seasons of the year.

The first farming communities in northern Europe did not build their superstructures in cities as we do today. They constructed large numbers of monuments in open ground. Some of these were great mounds of earth where they buried their dead. Others were places for religious and other ceremonies. In some cases, huge circles of land were enclosed by ditches and banks. This is how Stonehenge began, around 3000 BC. In other cases, the people stood large stone blocks in the ground, sometimes just one on its own, but often in circles or rows. We know, from evidence collected by archaeologists, how the people who built Stonehenge lived their lives. They plowed fields to grow crops such as wheat and barley, and also kept animals – cattle, sheep and goats. At first, their farm tools were made of stone, wood and bone, but when they discovered how to make things out of metals, such as bronze and gold, they were able to make much better tools, as well as beautiful objects and jewelry to wear.

▼ Raising the stones

The largest stones at Stonehenge are nearly 23 feet high and weigh over 45 tons. Standing them upright must have been extremely difficult and taken a huge number of people. The pictures below show one method the builders may have used to raise the monumental stones.

The structure of Stonehenge ▶

Inside the outer circle of stones was a smaller inner circle and two horseshoe arrangements of stones. The largest stones, known as sarsens, were brought from about 20 miles away. The smaller stones, known as bluestones, came from Welsh mountains over 125 miles away.

Circle of sarsen stones with lintels on the top

Horseshoe of sarsen stones

Circle of bluestones

Horseshoe of bluestones

Stonehenge today

Hundreds of thousands of people visit Stonehenge every year, and have done for centuries. Over the years some of the stones have fallen or been taken away. Even so, as a visiting archaeologist wrote in 1740, 'there is enough of every part to preserve the idea of the whole.'

◄ Skilful stonemasons

The builders of Stonehenge were skilful at fitting these huge stones together. They made the same sort of joints as are used in wood-working, where pegs in one piece of wood slot into the holes in another.

The lintels were linked by tongue and groove joints

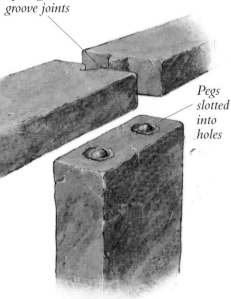

Pegs slotted into holes

▲ From the air

Stonehenge can be seen more clearly from the air. The view shows the stone circle enclosed by the bank and the ditch. Beyond the stone circle are two grassy banks – the ceremonial approach for processions to the site.

Tools ►

The people who built Stonehenge used earth-working tools made from the bones of animals. They used large hammers of hard sarsen stone to pound the stones into shape and make the joints.

Hammer stones

Antler pick

Bone shovel made from an ox blade

The Pyramids of Giza

Of the Seven Wonders of the Ancient World only one survives today – the Great Pyramid at Giza in northern Egypt. To construct this stone mountain, an army of workers moved and cut about 6.5 million tons of stone. The pyramid was built as a burial mound for Khufu, Pharaoh of Egypt. His mummified body was laid in a burial chamber, along with large numbers of objects for his life in the world beyond death.

The first-ever pyramid was designed in about 2700 BC by a court official named Imhotep for his master, the Pharaoh Djoser. Although Djoser's body was laid in a burial chamber deep under the ground, the pyramid rose 200 feet above the ground, and was built in a series of steps. The Pharaoh's family relatives and important officials were buried in much smaller tombs close to the royal pyramid. The favorite location was in the shadow of the pyramid itself. Imhotep's Step Pyramid is the oldest stone building of its size in the world. In later years, architects discovered how to build smooth-sided pyramids, like those at Giza. But from about 1550 BC, the age of pyramid-building drew to a close. Egyptian kings chose instead to be buried in tombs cut into the rock in the 'Land of the Dead' near Thebes.

◄ **The King and Queen**
The smallest of the three completed pyramids was the burial place of Pharaoh Menkaure. A number of statues were found close by, including this one of Menkaure and his queen, Khamerernebty II.

Anubis, God of Death ▶
The Egyptians believed that people lived on after death. The god Anubis weighed each person's heart against a feather to see whether they should live on with the gods or die a second death.

The pyramids at Giza
The Great Pyramid, the largest of them all, was first given the name 'Khufu is one belonging to the horizon'. The other large pyramids are the tombs of the Pharaohs Chephren and Menkaure. The two smaller pyramids were never completed. It is hard to believe that these ancient tombs lie a short distance from Cairo, capital of Egypt, and one of the fastest growing cities in the world.

▼ Mummification
The ancient Egyptians perfected the art of preserving bodies after death. This is called mummification. The bodies were packed in a salt called natron before being wrapped tightly in bandages.

Inside the Great Pyramid ▶
The Grand Gallery led to the burial chamber of the Pharaoh Khufu. Here, his mummified body was placed in a great stone coffin.

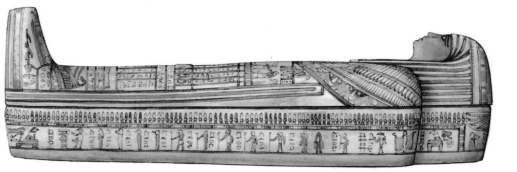

▲ Cutting the blocks

Huge blocks of limestone were split up by hammering wooden wedges into the rock, and pouring water down the cracks.

Building the Great Pyramid

It probably took 10,000 workers over 20 years to build the Great Pyramid. Archaeologists have found living quarters for about 4,000 specialist workers near the site.

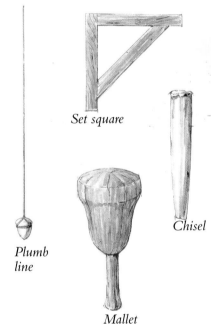

Set square

Chisel

Plumb line

Mallet

◀ A ramp to the top

Builders raised the heavy blocks on a ramp. As the pyramid grew higher, so too did the ramp. It was removed when the pyramid was finished.

◀ Tools

The pyramid builders worked with a variety of tools – some of which are still in use today. There were saws, drills, bronze chisels and mallets, and stones for pounding and polishing.

Foundations ▶

The site of the pyramid had to be perfectly level. It was cleared of sand down to the hard rock below.

◀ Transport by water

The stone for the pyramids was transported to the burial site along the River Nile. Rowing was the main means of powering the boats.

Saqqara 204 feet high

Meidum 302 feet high

Snefru Bent Pyramid 335 feet high

Abusir 331 feet high

The Great Pyramid
*Entry shafts were constructed
inside the pyramid to give
access to the burial
chambers. The shafts
were added while
the pyramid was
being built.*

Entrance

*Ascending
passage*

*Weight-relieving
chamber*

Entrance

The king ▶
*A statue of King Khufu.
By his time, Egyptian kings,
who owned the whole country
and had absolute power over
the people, took the title of
Pharaoh, which meant
'The Great House'.*

*King's burial
chamber*

Grand gallery

◀ The stone blocks
*The builders had to cut
about two and a half
million blocks of
stone, each weigh-
ing anything
from two to
fifteen tons.*

*Queen's burial
chamber*

*Ascending
passage*

Entrance

*Underground
chamber*

*Escape
route*

*Descending
corridor*

*Ground
level*

The facing stones ▶
*Smooth facing stones
were levered into position
to give the pyramid its
smooth shape.*

Pyramid of King Khafre 469 feet high

Great Pyramid 479 feet high

The Queen's Pyramids 200 feet high

The Acropolis

The Parthenon is the most famous ancient temple in the world. Its dazzling white marble columns must have towered over the ancient state of Athens, and can still be seen from many parts of the city today. The Parthenon is the largest of the temples on the Acropolis, a stony hill in the center of Athens, and was built in honor of Athene, the city's patron goddess. It was named after one of her titles – 'Parthenos', meaning 'the Virgin'. The building of the temple began in 447 BC, and took 15 years to complete.

Doric capital

Ionic capital

In early Greek times the town of Athens was one of several Greek states, each governed by its own king. By the 5th century BC the town had become the capital of a great empire, and had a population of about 250,000. By this time the Athenians had invented a special form of government called *demokratia*, which means democracy. All Athenian citizens (excluding women) came together about every nine days to discuss and vote on the decisions of the state. The ancient city of Athens was small by modern standards, but large areas of the town were set aside for worship, business and government. The Greeks were often at war, especially against the Persians, who invaded Greece several times. In 480 BC the Persian army captured Athens and destroyed all the buildings on the Acropolis. It was after this attack that the new temple to Athene was begun.

◀ Statue of Athene
Inside the Parthenon was a statue of Athene which stood about 43 feet high. The sculptor Pheidias carved her body from ivory and made her clothes of gold.

Stories in stone ▶
Inside and outside the Parthenon there were many carved panels which were originally brightly painted. This is a panel from a frieze showing the annual procession to honor and worship the goddess Athene.

The Parthenon today
Today only part of the Parthenon survives. In 1687, when it was being used to store gunpowder, a section of it was damaged in an explosion. In the 19th century, during the Turkish occupation of Greece, some of the sculptures were removed and later sold to the British Museum.

The Acropolis ▶

The 'High City', the Acropolis, was originally the stronghold of the early kings of Athens. It is a natural hill which was strengthened by stone walls. By the 5th century BC it had become the religious center of Athens. The other temples on the Acropolis include one to Athene in her role as the 'Victorious'.

The Classical style of architecture

Capital

Pediment

Doric
column

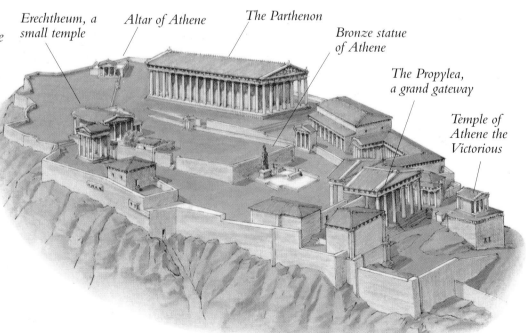

Erechtheum, a
small temple

Altar of Athene

The Parthenon

Bronze statue
of Athene

The Propylea,
a grand gateway

Temple of
Athene the
Victorious

The Great Wall of China

The Great Wall
Beijing
Hwang-Ho river
Yangtze river

China today is a huge single country with a population of over a billion people. But it was not always so unified. Over 2,000 years ago, in 221 BC, a new emperor called Ch'in Shi-huang-ti inherited a kingdom at war with itself. He pulled every part of it into one enormous country that was named China, after himself. He then ordered the construction of one of the wonders of the world – the Great Wall of China. Why was it great? Because it stretched for over 1,425 miles from the Yellow Sea in the east to central Asia in the west – a truly massive achievement.

Before the Emperor Ch'in came to the throne, China was divided into seven states, each with its own king. For 250 years the kings had been at war with each other and had built long walls of earth to protect their territory and keep out barbarian tribes to the north. Emperor Ch'in united the seven states and decided to make a single line of defense along the entire northern boundary. He joined the stretches of earth wall together and began to replace them with a stone wall studded with watch-towers. Ch'in Shi-huang-ti also reorganized the whole country, ordering a completely new system of roads and canals. He also established new nationwide laws, and systems of writings, money and weights and measures.

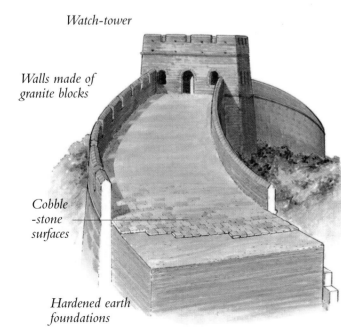

Watch-tower

Walls made of granite blocks

Cobble-stone surfaces

Hardened earth foundations

◄ Construction of the Great Wall
The Wall was first made of hardened earth. Later, brick or stone walls were added to make it 26 feet high. The top of the wall was paved with cobblestones, and it was wide enough for five horsemen to ride side by side.

Construction workers ►
The workers included soldiers, criminals and able-bodied men who were working as a form of taxation. Thousands died of cold or from the cruelty of their overseers.

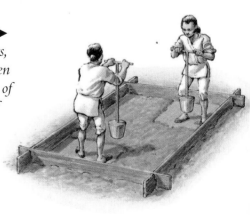

▲ A formidable defense

The Great Wall twists and snakes its way across mountainous countryside. It was almost impossible for China's enemies to get into the country. The Wall was guarded by watch-towers and defended gateways. There were also 10,000 lamps to warn patrolling soldiers of an attack.

Chinese wheelbarrow ▶

The Chinese invented all sorts of things we still use today, including the wheelbarrow. Construction workers on the Wall were using the wheelbarrow 1,000 years before it was seen in the West. They called it the 'wooden ox'.

The Great Wall

Huang-Ho river

Beijing

Yellow river

Yellow Sea

Chang'an (Xian)

Louyong

Chengdu

Yangtze river

0   300   500 miles

Extent of the Ch'in Empire

17

Tomb of the Emperor Ch'in

One of the most remarkable discoveries from the ancient world is the tomb of the Chinese emperor, Ch'in Shihuang-ti. In 212 BC the all-powerful emperor began a massive building program. A Chinese historian recorded how the emperor forced 700,000 laborers, most of them convicts, to build a palace at Xianyang and to work on a tomb on Mount Li. The tomb, which took nearly 40 years to construct, lies under a huge mound of earth, over 15,000 square feet.

The ancient Chinese believed that, after death, people lived a similar life to the one they had just lived. Because of this, dead people were buried with all their worldly possessions, so that these would be useful to them in their next life. In early times, the Chinese had killed and buried servants alongside their masters and mistresses, so that they could continue to serve them in the next world. By the time of the Emperor Ch'in, this custom had died out and, instead of real corpses, pottery models were buried in the tombs. To serve the emperor and guard the entrance to his tomb, there was a vast army of over 7,000 pottery figures. The models filled three huge burial pits, which lie less than a mile from the emperor himself. The tomb is more like a palace, constructed under a huge mound of earth, which lies inside a great courtyard surrounded by walls. When the tomb was complete, the emperor is said to have ordered the killing of everyone who knew where it was and what it contained. Even so, the burial pits were soon plundered after he died.

▲ The Emperor Ch'in
A Chinese writer remarked that the Emperor had 'a waspish nose, eyes like slits, a chicken breast and a voice like a jackal'.

A vast army ▶
The pottery models included footsoldiers, bowmen, spearmen and officers. Each one was life-size and had a different face. The figures were painted to make them look more lifelike.

▲ Horses

Hundreds of pottery horses were buried to pull the chariots and carry the cavalry. Each one had a leather bridle and a metal bit.

Covering earth mound

Ground level

Layers of plaster and fiber matting

Wooden posts

Armored soldiers

Horse-drawn chariots

Crossbowmen

Brick path

The burial pits ▲

The three burial pits have been named Pit 1, 2 and 3 in order of size. In Pit 1 the pottery army was placed in battle formation, on a brick floor between walls of earth. Wooden beams formed a roof over the corridors.

Pit 1 ►

Main army: 6,000 foot soldiers, 702 crossbowmen, 30 chariots and horses

◄ Pit 3

Command post: commander, officers, guards, 64 figures and chariots

◄ Pit 2

Cavalry: 1,400 soldiers, 89 chariots and 360 horses

▲ A model soldier

Each pottery figure was modeled wearing armor. The soldiers carried real weapons, such as spears and swords. This one originally carried a crossbow.

The City of Petra

The word 'Petra' means 'rock', and this is just the right name for a remarkable city, nestled in the mountains and literally built out of rock. In ancient times, travelers to Petra had to squeeze through gaps in a gorge, just as tourists do today, to reach the flatter, more open area where the city was built. High cliffs rise all around the city, and some of its buildings were actually carved out of the rock. Today, Petra lies in the country of Jordan, but when it was built it was the capital city of a people called the Nabateans.

The Nabateans originally came from northern Arabia. They made their living by farming and trade. One of the most important trades was that of incense, a sticky gum produced by trees in the area. Different gums were burnt as incense in religious ceremonies, used for embalming the dead, or added to perfumes or cosmetics. Frankincense and myrrh are two kinds of incense, and were among the gifts offered to the Christ child. These and other incenses were much in demand.

Petra lay at the crossroads between the Roman world to the west and India to the east. The city was an important trading center, receiving shipments from Red Sea ports and bustling with merchants and camel trains. As well as incense, there was trading in cloth such as silk, damask and cotton, spices such as ginger and pepper, and precious objects made from silver, gold and glass.

◀ The city streets
The Romans conquered Petra in AD 106. They added a theatre and a long street lined with colonnades – rows of columns which once supported a roof over the walkways on either side.

God of the mountains ▶
The Nabateans built this temple, in the 1st century BC, for the worship of Dushara, one of their principal gods. Dushara was represented in the temple by a block of stone.

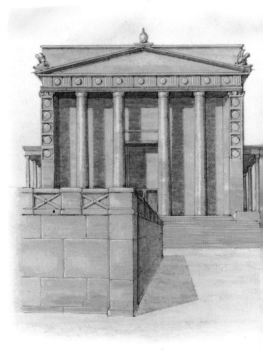

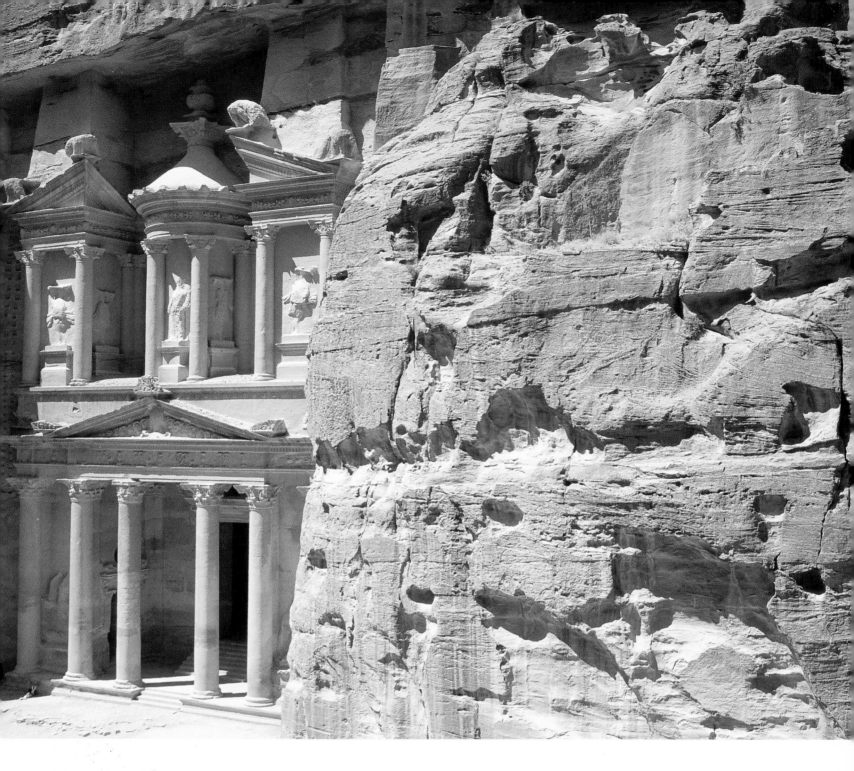

▲ The Khazneh

The most amazing structures at Petra are rock-cut tombs, such as this one, called the Khazneh. The outside of the tomb was carved from the top downwards. This Khazneh was probably for Aretas III, a Nabatean king who ruled from 86 to 62 BC.

Inside a tomb ▶

The facade, or front, of the Khazneh tomb has many elaborate carvings. Visitors pass between the four columns into a square hall which was probably used for religious ceremonies. At the back of the tomb lie three burial chambers.

◀ *Detail from the facade*

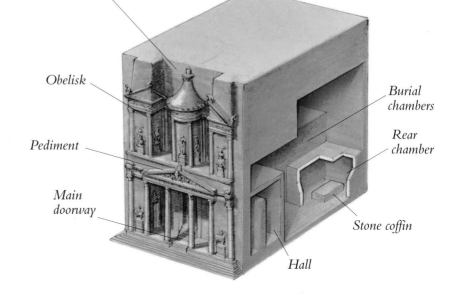

Facade of carved sandstone

Obelisk

Pediment

Main doorway

Hall

Burial chambers

Rear chamber

Stone coffin

21

The Forum of Rome

Perugia

Orvieto

Rome
The Forum

Naples

At the center of all Roman cities lay a large open square called the forum. This is where the most important public buildings were to be found. In the *Forum Romanum* – the forum of the city of Rome – were the buildings of government, religion and business, and commemorations of Roman victory in war. The forum was the heart of the city – the venue for important public ceremonies such as religious or state processions, and the meeting place for people in business.

Arch of Titus

Temple of Vesta

The beginning of Rome lies shrouded in legend. The Romans believed that their city had been founded around 753 BC by twin boys called Romulus and Remus. The brothers had been abandoned as babies, saved by a she-wolf and raised by a humble shepherd. Over the years the Romans expanded their territory beyond the city. By the second century AD, they controlled a huge empire, which stretched from Britain to Syria and from Germany to North Africa and had a population of between 50 and 60 million people. For 500 years Rome was governed by elected officials, but then powerful politicians took over. The first emperor, Augustus, came to power in 31 BC. At his death, he boasted that 'I found the city of Rome built of sun-dried bricks. I leave her covered in marble.' Over the centuries more and more buildings were added to the Roman Forum until there was barely room for the public processions!

◄ The forum today
2,000 years later, only ruins survive in the Forum Romanum. The three tall columns on the right were part of an enormous temple which was also used for meetings of the senate – the government of Rome.

The Emperor Augustus ▶
This is a marble statue of Augustus when he was about 45 years old. He is shown in the full uniform of an army general.

Temple of Romulus

Temple of Castor and Pollux

Temple of Julius Caesar

Basilica Maxentius

▲ The Arch of Septimius Severus

This ceremonial arch was ordered by Emperor Septimius Severus who reigned in the 3rd century AD. It commemorates the defeat of the Parthians and the extension of the Roman Empire in the east.

Forum Romanum ▶

1 Triumphal arch of Septimius Severus
2 Platform where politicians addressed meetings
3 The curia, the meeting place of the senate
4 and 5 Basilicas were large buildings used as law courts, for business and social gatherings
6 Temple of Vesta, the goddess of hearth and home
7 Temple of Romulus
8 Temple of Venus (goddess of love) and Roma
9 Temple of Castor and Pollux, twin sons of Jupiter, king of the gods
10 Temple of Julius Caesar
11 Temple of the Emperor Antoninus and his wife Faustina
12 The Sacred Way, used for processions
13 The Colosseum

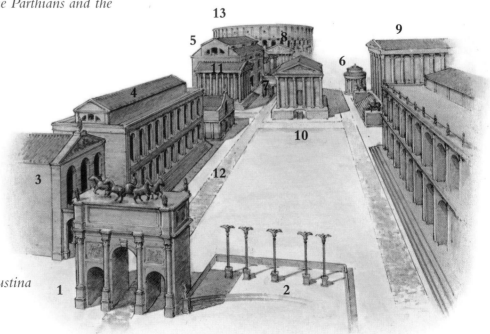

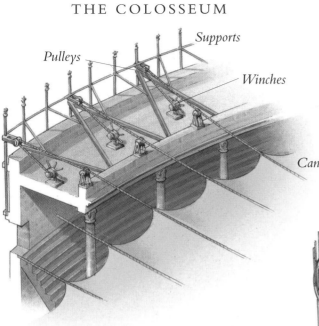

Supports

Pulleys

Winches

Canopy

▲ The canopy

Shows at the Colosseum lasted all day. To shade spectators from the burning sun, a huge canopy could be drawn right over the building. On the top level of the arena, 165 feet above the ground, hundreds of workers turned 80 winches. Slowly but surely, a huge rope and canvas cover called a valerium was hoisted over the arena.

▼ Roman engineering

To construct huge buildings like the Colosseum, the Romans needed to be skilled at accurate surveying and in inventing ingenious machinery. This large wooden crane was powered by men working a treadmill. It could lift heavy blocks of stone high into the air.

▼ The Colosseum

This huge amphitheatre was built to hold public entertainments for the people of Rome, and could seat up to 50,000 spectators. The building was completed by the Emperor Titus in AD 80, and was named after a colossal statue of the Emperor Nero, which stood nearby.

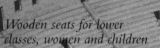

Canopy

Wooden seats for lower classes, women and children

Seats for the middle classes

Seats for high-ranking people

Seats for Roman officials

Arena

▲ Watching the games

Spectators poured through 80 entrances to watch the free shows put on for them by the emperor. In the morning there were fights with wild beasts. At lunch-time criminals were executed or made to fight each other to the death. In the afternoon the gladiators fought each other, usually to the death.

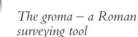

The groma – a Roman surveying tool

Underground vaults ▶

The wooden floor of the Colosseum was laid over vaults built of brick. These formed a complicated network of under-ground tunnels, work and storage rooms.

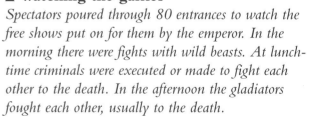

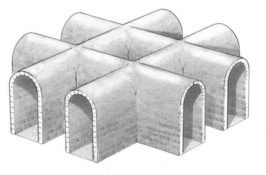

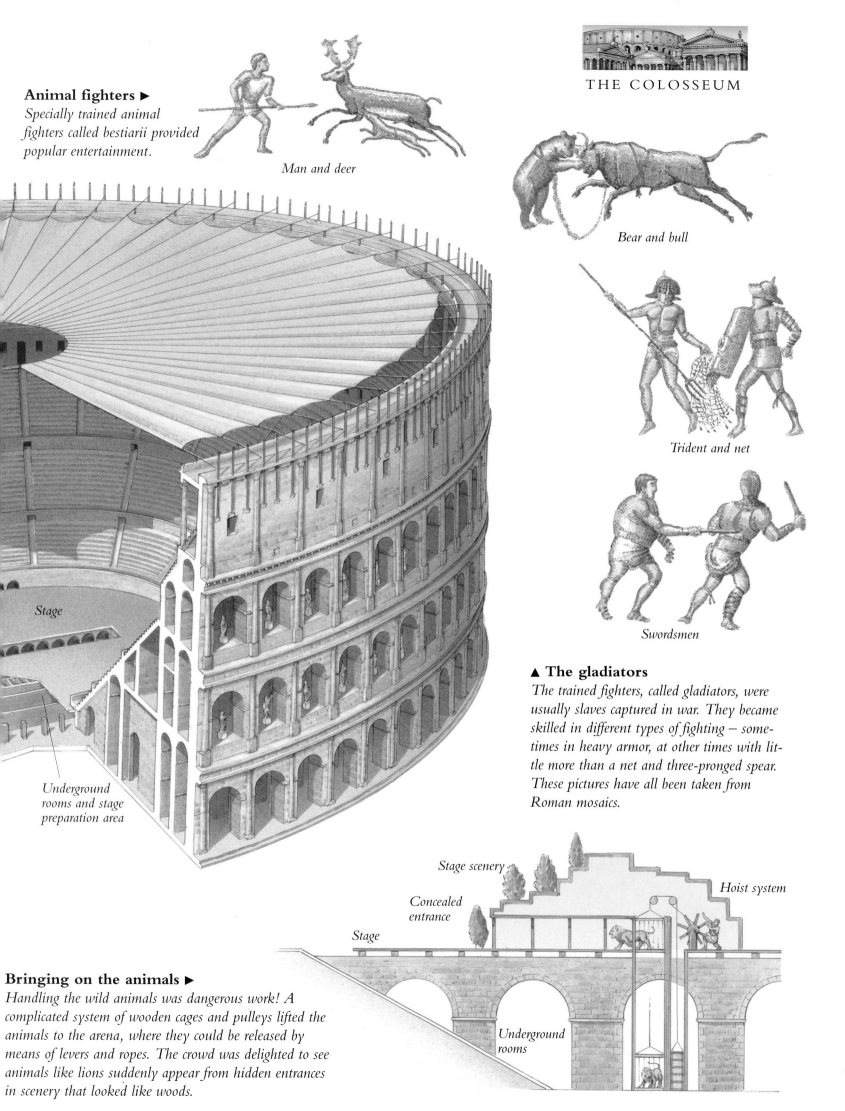

Animal fighters ▶
Specially trained animal fighters called bestiarii provided popular entertainment.

Man and deer

Bear and bull

Trident and net

Swordsmen

Stage

Underground rooms and stage preparation area

▲ The gladiators
The trained fighters, called gladiators, were usually slaves captured in war. They became skilled in different types of fighting – sometimes in heavy armor, at other times with little more than a net and three-pronged spear. These pictures have all been taken from Roman mosaics.

Stage scenery

Concealed entrance

Hoist system

Stage

Underground rooms

Bringing on the animals ▶
Handling the wild animals was dangerous work! A complicated system of wooden cages and pulleys lifted the animals to the arena, where they could be released by means of levers and ropes. The crowd was delighted to see animals like lions suddenly appear from hidden entrances in scenery that looked like woods.

25

Mesa Verde

The south-western corner of North America is a rugged, mountainous land of peaks, canyons and cliffs. Around AD 1100, the Anasazi people began building along the sides of the canyons, in the shelter of overhanging cliffs. They constructed huge houses from the sandstone rocks, and made mortar from local mud. This area was the land of the mesas – steep, high-sided hills with flat tops – and had been home to people for hundreds of years.

The Anasazi cliff-dwellers were farmers. They kept turkeys, and grew crops such as maize, squashes and beans on the flat land above their houses, irrigating their fields during long periods of drought. But they were also hunters, and varied their diet with squirrel, rat and deer meat, as well as with eggs and fruit. All their food was stored and cooked in colorfully decorated clay pots. They were able craftspeople, sewing animal skins into bags, weaving cotton into cloth, and using the fibers of the yucca plant to make blankets and socks. Around 1300, the village at Mesa Verde was completely abandoned. This followed 20 years of drought, when there was little to eat and nothing to sow. Perhaps the final straw for the Anasazi was fierce attacks by other hunters in the region, ancestors of the modern Navajo and Apache peoples.

◀ **Four-story houses**
Some of the buildings were like blocks of apartments up to four stories high. The Anasazi were well protected by the cliff, but they also built watch-towers for extra security.

Woven water jar lined with pitch

The houses at Mesa Verde were often grouped around a courtyard. These may have been communal areas where people prepared food or made tools and other household objects. In the front of the picture is an underground room called a kiva.

Underground rooms ▶

The Anasazi built special circular underground rooms, called kivas. These were meeting rooms for religious and other ceremonies and could only be used by men. A hole in the floor, called a sipapu, was thought to be the entrance to the spirit world.

Plastered roof supported by beams

Stone block construction, bound with mud mortar

Hearth

Sipapu

▼ Anasazi jewelry

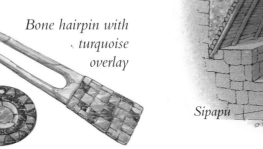

Bone hairpin with turquoise overlay

Turquoise mosaic earrings

Chartres Cathedral

Chartres, the best-preserved medieval cathedral in France, boasts impressive architecture, beautiful stained glass and intricate sculpture. The cathedral you see today was begun in 1194, but it was 26 years later before there was a roof over the building. Other cathedrals had been built on this site over the past 450 years. During that time, fires and Viking attacks had destroyed no fewer than four cathedrals, and the town of Chartres itself.

In the medieval world, religion was an important part of everyday life. A Christian church was built for each community. The shape and architecture of each church varied enormously throughout Europe. Cathedrals were 'houses for God', built to allow large congregations of people to come together in worship. At the time of the first cathedral in Chartres, and for centuries afterwards, cathedrals looked very heavy, with large round arches and thick columns. But by the middle of the 12th century a completely new style of architecture was developing, called the Gothic style. Builders wanted higher and lighter cathedrals, and their buildings were quite different from anything seen before. At Chartres, they built a cathedral that was much brighter than the dark, rather forbidding cathedrals of the past. As one writer of the time put it, the cathedral was filled with a 'new light', which the priests compared to the light of heaven.

◄ The Rose Window
The 'new light' streamed into Chartres through beautiful stained glass windows. It would have taken six skilled glaziers two or three years to complete a window like this.

Medieval craftspeople ►
Hundreds of workers were needed to build Chartres cathedral. Often, groups of specialized workers, such as stonemasons, formed themselves into guilds. Here, a laborer prepares a load of lime mortar.

A view of Chartres showing its most striking feature – its ill-matched spires. The smaller south spire (on the right) was completed by about 1160, and is plain and conical in design. The taller north spire (on the left) was not built until the 16th century, and reflects a much more decorative style.

CHARTRES CATHEDRAL

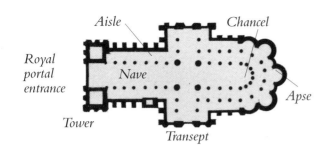

Aisle

Chancel

Royal portal entrance

Nave

Apse

Tower

Transept

▲ Cathedral plan

Churches and cathedrals had a place for the congregation (the nave) and a place for the priest to conduct the service (the chancel). Cathedrals were built in the shape of a cross, to signify the cross on which Jesus was crucified.

Building in stone ▶

In medieval times most buildings were made of wood. But the more important buildings, like cathedrals, churches, palaces and castles, were constructed in stone. This meant that they were expensive to build and usually took years to complete.

Flying buttress

Clerestory

Upper story

Flying buttress

◀ Flying buttresses

Towering columns lifted the roof higher and provided more space inside the cathedral. This was possible because of a new building technique called the 'flying buttress'. Flying buttresses supported the weight of the building on columns and arches outside the cathedral walls.

A mason's tools

Master masons ▶

Masons (stone-cutters) were in great demand for their skills. A master mason might work with about 30 experienced workers, traveling from job to job. They produced stone blocks, carved columns and window moldings. But that was not all. Chartres cathedral is full of wonderful sculptures both inside and out. The example on the left shows St John the Baptist from the North Porch of the cathedral.

30

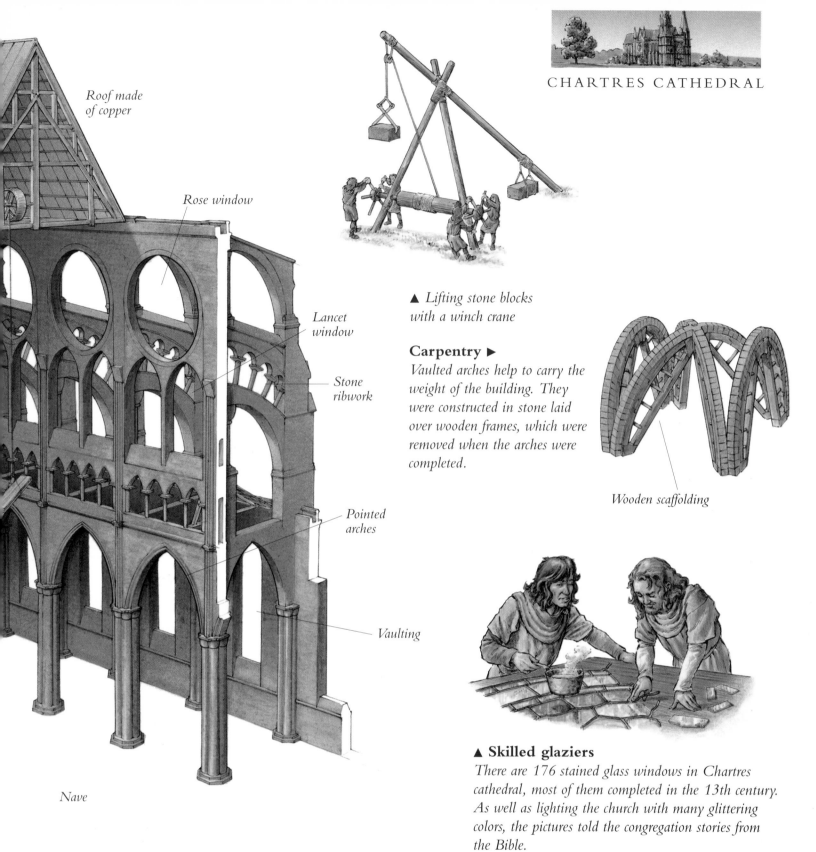

Roof made of copper

Rose window

Lancet window

Stone ribwork

Pointed arches

Vaulting

Nave

▲ *Lifting stone blocks with a winch crane*

Carpentry ▶
Vaulted arches help to carry the weight of the building. They were constructed in stone laid over wooden frames, which were removed when the arches were completed.

Wooden scaffolding

▲ Skilled glaziers
There are 176 stained glass windows in Chartres cathedral, most of them completed in the 13th century. As well as lighting the church with many glittering colors, the pictures told the congregation stories from the Bible.

▼ Stained glass windows
Taurus the Bull – a detail from the Signs of the Zodiac window

Pisces the Fish

A detail from the parable of the Good Samaritan

The Last Supper

The City of Venice

Venice is one of the most amazing cities in the world. What makes it unique is that it was built on a hundred or more islands inside a marshy lagoon. Elegant buildings have been constructed on the islands, and canals now form the main thoroughfares of the city. During the Middle Ages, Venice was the world's most successful port, an important link between East and West. Today, 120,000 people live in this city on the sea.

By 1250, Venice's population had reached 90,000. Its merchants traded all around the Mediterranean Sea and established colonies, for example on Crete, to encourage their business. By the end of the century, their ships were sailing to the Black Sea, Syria and Egypt, along the north African coast, and to Spain and France. The Venetian traders grew wealthy and built sumptuous palaces for their homes. They would buy a hundred-weight of pepper for three ducats in India, and sell it in Europe for 80!

◀ The Doge

The city of Venice was more like a state. It was governed by a senate and a Grand Council. The ruler of Venice was called the Doge, a respectable man aged about 70 or more, from one of the greatest Venetian families. The Doge could be identified by the hat he wore, which had a rounded peak woven in gold and silver and covered with precious stones.

▼ The rise of Venice

The picture comes from a 16th-century manuscript and shows what Venice's first settlements may have looked like. The timber-framed houses have walls of dried mud and roofs of thatched reeds.

So many people lived in medieval Venice that the houses were built very close together and several stories high. The city's wealth was displayed in its many fine churches and public squares.

The Arsenal ▶

The city authorities built a huge shipyard called the Arsenal, in which ships were built and maintained. About 2,000 shipyard workers called arsenalotti constructed all sorts of craft, from light warships to heavy merchant galleys. They worked so fast that they could build a galley in a week. The Arsenal also made ropes, which were stored in great warehouses along the quays.

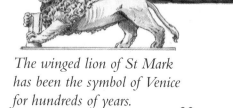

The winged lion of St Mark has been the symbol of Venice for hundreds of years.

THE CITY OF VENICE

◄ Island city
Venice began as a small port, but in the early Middle Ages its population began to grow. Over the years, more and more muddy land was reclaimed for building, and smaller islands were joined to form larger areas of land. Nevertheless about 120 islands still make up the city today.

Palatial palazzos ►
The house of an important merchant or banking family was called a palazzo or palace. Palazzos were usually divided into three stories. The ground floor had a grand entrance but also shops or storage space. The second floor was for offices and archives. The top floor was where the family lived, while the servants slept in the attic.

▲ Pile driving
Venice's buildings rest on foundations of sharp wooden posts called piles. These were driven down through the muddy water into a layer of clay up to 100 feet below. If the water was deeper than this, it had to be drained off before work on the foundations could begin.

▼ On the roof
Kitchens were located in the attic space of the palazzo. Elaborately-decorated chimneys were built on the roof. This upside-down bell shape was especially common.

Attic

Top floor

Second floor

Ground floor

Foundations

Piles

Clay

◄ Firm foundations
Above the wooden piles, builders laid a lattice-work of timber, stone and mortar, which provided a firm foundation for the house above. The walls of the building were made of brick, while heavy stonework was restricted to decorative touches around the doors and windows.

Doge's Palace

Palazzo Calergi

Palazzo Centanni

Palazzo da Mula

Palazzo Barbarigo

▼ The Grand Canal

The main thoroughfare of Venice is the Grand Canal. About 150 smaller waterways run off it. In medieval Venice, everything and everyone was transported by boat, and that is still true of the city today.

▼ The gondola

Flat-bottomed boats called gondolas transport people and goods through the city. Gondolas are highly decorated and are steered by gondoliers, who work a single wooden oar at the stern.

◀ Venetian craftspeople

Medieval Venice was famous for the quality of its craftwork — especially stonecarving, glass and mosaic making.

▲ Bridges

About 400 bridges connect the islands of Venice.

The growth of Venice ▶

Venice grew steadily during the Middle Ages. As well as the densely-packed houses, there were many churches, bell towers, guild houses and other grand buildings, which were used for the government of the city and its huge trading empire.

Moorings ▶

Wooden posts called palines are used to moor the boats. Bright colors and stripes show which family the moorings belong to.

Palazzo Gritti

Ca' d'oro

Palazzo Pesaro

Ca' Rezzonico

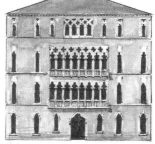

Palazzo Bernado Grimani

Great Zimbabwe

This extraordinary complex of stone buildings, walls and towers was once a capital city in Africa in the country we now call Zimbabwe. The ancient city dates from the 12th century, and is called Great Zimbabwe because it is the grandest settlement from this period of history. Its original name is unknown. By about AD 1350 Great Zimbabwe was the residence of the most powerful ruler in south-eastern Africa and had a population of more than 10,000 people.

People had lived on the site of Great Zimbabwe for many centuries in houses of wood and clay, but it was not until around AD 1200 that a larger settlement was founded with houses of stone. The people who moved to Great Zimbabwe were cattle farmers, who needed large areas of land to graze their cattle. Powerful leaders organized the people into herding and guarding the cattle, and protecting their lands from attack. Great Zimbabwe was built on a natural stone hill and stretched to the flat plains below. Yet it seems that its massive stone walls were built only to impress. There is no sign of walls around the outside of the city to defend it from attack. Many skilled workers lived in the city – builders, sculptors, metal-workers, jewelers, weavers and potters. Most of the people ate meat. Although they grew grain, it was used mainly to brew their beer.

◄ Religious carvings
This bird is skillfully carved from a soft stone, called soapstone. Images of birds and animals were displayed on wooden or stone poles and were probably an important part of people's beliefs about their ancestors.

Stone doorways ►
It took great skill to build in stone. This is the only doorway to survive in its original condition. The top of the doorway has a stone beam which supports the wall above. Other doorways may have been built with a beam of wood instead.

▲ The Great Enclosure

The high walls of the Great Enclosure were built from a million blocks of granite stone. Inside, there probably lived five or six families, related to the king. They too had stone houses inside their own private enclosures.

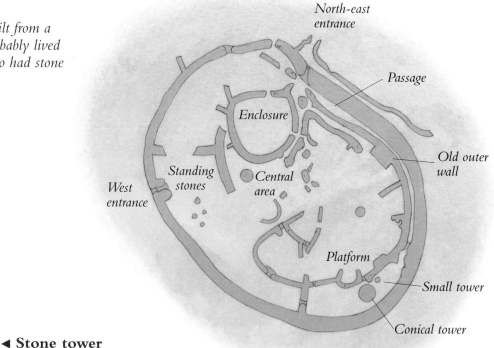

North-east entrance

Passage

Enclosure

Standing stones

West entrance

Central area

Old outer wall

Platform

Small tower

Conical tower

◀ Stone tower

Inside the Great Enclosure stands this solid tower of stone, nearly 33 feet high. Archaeologists think that it represents the power of the king who probably lived close by.

In the Shona language the word 'zimbabwe' comes from either 'dzimba dza mabwe' ('houses of stone') or 'dzimba woye' ('chief's houses'). Great Zimbabwe must have been the royal residence. Its narrow, winding entrances ensured that the courtyards and houses remained very private.

Machu Picchu

High in the Andes Mountains in Peru in South America lies a deserted stone city called Machu Picchu. This was a city of the Incas, and lay not far from their capital city of Cuzco. Machu Picchu was founded sometime after AD 1438 and about 1,000 people lived there. Their city was a real fortress, defended by sheer drops on three sides and a deep, dry moat and high stone walls on the fourth. Within the city, more than 3,000 steps linked its houses, temples and palaces.

Around AD 1200 the Incas were still a small tribe, but they expanded to become an enormous empire of about eight million people. By the 15th century they ruled a kingdom that stretched across an area from Ecuador to Chile. The Incas called their empire Tahuantinsuyu, which means the 'Land of the Four Quarters'. They were ruled by an emperor known as Sapa Inca, which means 'the only emperor'. The emperor appointed a governor to rule each quarter of the empire. The Incas were excellent engineers, and built over 14,250 miles of paved roads throughout their empire. They turned a land of mountains, jungles and desert coasts into a rich country. Most Incas were farmers, growing maize, beans, chili peppers, avocados, potatoes and peanuts. They also kept pigs and ducks, llamas to carry their goods and alpacas for their soft, warm wool.

Counting by knots ▶
The Incas kept records and accounts by counting in tens on a quipu. This was made of colored cords, tied with single, double or treble knots.

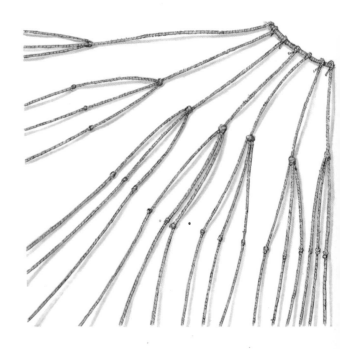

◀ City plan
The builders of Machu Picchu made a clay or stone model before they constructed the city. A large open area, called he plaza, was where public meetings took place or announcements were made.

Plaza

Temple

Storehouses

Prison

Palace

Burial caves

Town gate

Barracks

Agricultural terraces

High in the Andes lies the fortress-city of Machu Picchu. It was built during the reign of Emperor Pachacuti Inca Yupanqui, who extended the Inca empire across present-day Peru. The Spaniards conquered and destroyed this great civilization in 1532.

◄ Earthquake protection

The stone walls were not stuck together with mortar because of the frequent earth tremors in this part of the world. Without mortar, the stones could move a little without the walls breaking up.

Building in stone ►

The Incas were skilful builders. They cut and shaped granite using hammers made from a hard material called obsidian. The blocks were made so accurately that you can hardly see the cracks in between them.

The Taj Mahal

In 1631, Mumtaz Mahal, the wife of the Emperor of India, died after giving birth to her fourteenth child. The Emperor Shah Jehan was said to be so grief-stricken that he 'would no longer listen to music or singing and would not wear fine linen clothes. He was forced to use spectacles because of his constant weeping.' He planned to build the world's most beautiful memorial to his beloved wife, and in 1642 the mausoleum was complete. It was called the Taj Mahal, which means the 'Crown of Palaces'.

The Emperor Shah Jehan was one of the Mughal rulers of India, descended from the Mongol conqueror, Genghis Khan. The title 'Shah Jehan' means 'World Ruler' and the man was certainly ruthless. He is said to have murdered most of his relatives to inherit the throne in 1628. Like other Muslim rulers, he kept a harem of wives, but Mumtaz Mahal from Persia was his greatest love – indeed her name means 'The Chosen One of the Palace'. The Taj Mahal was not the only building project undertaken by the emperor. His capital city, Agra, was near to the Taj Mahal, along the River Yamuna. He ordered many of the buildings in Agra to be covered with glowing white sheets of marble. His own architects were employed to design the mausoleum, but designers and artists were also hired from all over his empire and beyond.

▲ Emperor and Empress
Portraits of Shah Jehan and Mumtaz Mahal. The Emperor had intended to build another mausoleum for himself made of black marble, but it was never built. Instead he was buried next to his favorite wife.

Inside the mausoleum ▶
The inside of Mumtaz Mahal's tomb was as highly decorated as the outside. The burial place of the Empress and Emperor was marked by cenotaphs and surrounded by a carved marble screen (detail below).

The gleaming white marble of the Taj Mahal contrasts with the green gardens, and is reflected in the stillness of the pool. In fact, the mausoleum was built of stone rubble – the marble is only a veneer!

◄ Inlaid marble

Pictures of flowers decorate the Taj Mahal. It took great skill to produce intricate designs like the one below – cutting thin pieces of marble so accurately that they fitted together perfectly. Precious stones were also used to decorate the walls.

Marble inlaid with semi-precious stones

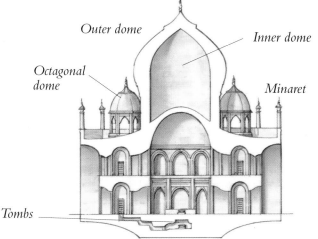

Outer dome

Inner dome

Octagonal dome

Minaret

Tombs

▲ It took ten years to complete the mausoleum, and another 12 years to finish the gardens and surrounding buildings. As many as 20,000 people helped to build the Taj Mahal. A town called Mumtazabad grew up to accommodate them while they worked on the site.

41

The Hoover Dam

At its completion in 1936, the Hoover Dam was the new modern wonder of the world. It was taller than the Great Pyramid and took more manpower than the Colosseum. What was it for? A dam is a barrier built across a river to hold back the water. The water that collects can then be used to provide water for drinking and for irrigation. The energy of flowing water can also be used to generate electricity and provide hydro-electric power.

People have been building dams since the earliest civilizations. We know that a dam was constructed across the River Nile in Egypt in about 2900 BC to protect the city of Memphis from flooding. In modern times, many large dams have been built throughout the world to provide electricity. There are about 50,000 dams in the United States alone. The Hoover Dam, named after President Herbert Hoover, is constructed across the Colorado river. In 1900, as the population in south-west America began to grow, a new dam was needed to provide electricity. After many years of discussions and debates, work finally began in 1931, and on September 11, 1936, President Roosevelt pushed the button to start the generator. By October 9, electricity was being generated for the farming communities in the surrounding area.

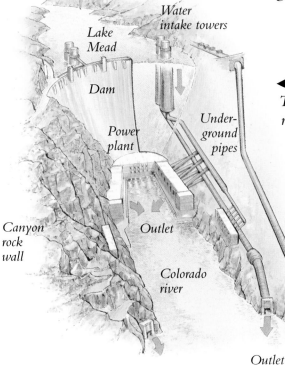

◄ How the dam was built
The first job was to divert the Colorado river. Four tunnels were dug, each about ¾ mile long. With the water diverted, work on the foundations for the dam could begin.

Water was allowed to flow from ► the lake above the dam through huge steel pipes – some over 30 feet in diameter – to the power plant below. In all, 838 miles of pipework was used in the construction of the dam.

▲ The site
The dam's towering concrete wall holds back an artificial lake called Lake Mead, which extends more than 105 miles behind the dam.

◄ A concrete bath
The massive dam wall is 725 feet high. It was built by filling a wooden 'mold' with over three million buckets of wet concrete! This took two years to complete.

▲ Working on site
A complete town was built to accommodate the 1,300 construction workers. It was called Boulder City and had its own schools, police force and fire department. This photograph was taken in 1934.

Glossary

acropolis The highest point in a Greek town, usually defended.

apse Half-rounded end of a church or cathedral.

archaeologist A scientist who collects and interprets evidence from the past which survives in buildings, or on or under the ground.

cenotaph A monument to a dead person.

chancel The part of a church or cathedral where the priest conducts the service.

clerestory The upper part of a church or cathedral with a series of windows.

Doge The ruler of Venice.

dome A rounded top on a building or room.

empire A large territory, usually covering more than one country, ruled over by an emperor or king.

flying buttress An arch-shaped support built on the outside of a cathedral to carry the enormous weight of the walls and roof.

forum The open market square of a Roman town. Most public buildings were grouped around the forum.

gladiator Professional fighter in Roman amphitheatres who fought against each other or wild animals – usually to the death.

gondola A long, narrow, flat-bottomed boat, used to transport people and goods on the canals of Venice.

hydro-electric power Power generated by the force of falling water.

kiva Underground room used by Anasazi men for religious meetings.

mason A skilled craftsperson who cuts and carves stone for buildings.

mausoleum A fine stone building for the burial of an important or rich person.

mortar A mixture of materials, such as lime, sand and water, to hold bricks and stones together.

mosaic Wall or floor decoration made up of many small fragments of stone, tile or glass.

mummification The process of drying and preserving a body, used by the ancient Egyptians and others.

nave The part of a church or cathedral where the congregation stands or sits.

palazzo Palace or grand house in Italy in the Middle Ages.

Pharaoh The title for an Egyptian king from about 1350 BC, meaning 'The Great House'.

plaza Large open area in the center of early American towns.

pyramid A tomb for an Egyptian king. It is named after its shape.

quipu Knotted cords used by the Incas for counting and keeping records.

sarsen Type of stone used to build the largest constructions at Stonehenge.

sipapu A hole cut in the floor of a kiva, thought to be the entrance to the spirit world.

treadmill A large wheel turned by people or animals to power a crane.

vault One or more arches built so that they form a roof.

Index

THE ACROPOLIS

THE CITY OF VENICE

THE TAJ MAHAL

STONEHENGE

CHARTRES CATHEDRAL

THE FORUM OF ROME

THE CITY OF PETRA

GREAT ZIMBABWE

THE PYRAMIDS OF GIZA